I want to be a Teacher

I WANT TO BE A
Teacher

DAN LIEBMAN

FIREFLY BOOKS

A FIREFLY BOOK

Published by Firefly Books Ltd. 2018

First Printing, 2018

Library of Congress Control Number: 2018934048

Library and Archives Canada Cataloguing in Publication
Liebman, Daniel, author
     I want to be a teacher / Dan Liebman.
Previously published: Willowdale, Ontario: Firefly Books, 2001.
ISBN 978-0-228-10145-1 (hardcover).--ISBN 978-0-228-10102-4 (softcover)
     1. Teachers--Juvenile literature. 2. Teaching--Vocational guidance--
Juvenile literature. I. Title. II. Title: Teacher.
LB1775.L535 2018   j371.1   C2018-901024-X

Published in Canada by
Firefly Books Ltd.
50 Staples Avenue, Unit 1
Richmond Hill, Ontario L4B 0A7

Published in the United States by
Firefly Books (U.S.) Inc.
P.O. Box 1338, Ellicott Station
Buffalo, New York, USA 14205

Photo Credits
© Monkey Business Images /Shutterstock.com, front
   cover, back cover, pages 5-6, 9, 21
© sirtravelalot/Shutterstock.com, page 7
© Tyler Olson/Shutterstock.com, page 8
© GG Pro Photo/Shutterstock.com, page 10
© Africa Studio/Shutterstock.com, page 11
© goodluz/Shutterstock.com, pages 12, 16
© wavebreakmedia/Shutterstock.com, pages 13–14, 18

© Rawpixel.com/Shutterstock.com, page 15
© mastapiece/Shutterstock.com, pages 17
© dotshock/Shutterstock.com, page 19
© alexkatkov/Shutterstock.com, page 20
© antoniodiaz/Shutterstock.com, page 22
© SpeedKingz/Shutterstock.com, page 23
© Rawpixel.com/Shutterstock.com, page 24

Design by Interrobang Graphic Design Inc.
Printed and bound in China

 *We acknowledge the financial support of the Government of Canada.*

Teachers work hard to make their classes interesting.

Art class can be fun for everyone.

Reading time is an important part of the day.

This teacher uses his hands and his face to tell a story to children who are deaf.

Teachers like to help students one at a time.

This teacher explains that there are different ways to count. This girl is using an abacus.

Teachers help students use computers to learn.

They also spend time helping children with their homework.

In this shop class, students learn to work safely.

These students want to be gymnasts. Their teacher is helping them train.

Teachers also help after school. This music teacher is in charge of band practice.

This ballet teacher is showing her students how to dance.

Some teachers give private music lessons.